Chartreux Cats

A Pet Care Guide for Chartreux Cats

Chartreux Cat Breed General Info, Purchasing, Care, Cost, Keeping, Health, Supplies, Food, Breeding and More Included!

By Lolly Brown

Copyrights and Trademarks

Disclaimer and Legal Notice

Foreword

Picture this: a nice, calm cat sits beside you on the couch on a sunny morning. It has a beautiful woolly coat and deep copper eyes staring not at you, but at that little toy you're holding out, and then, it does the most amazing thing… it swiftly fetches the toy and returns to your side with what looks like a smile on its face. If you liked what you saw, then the Chartreux Cat is the perfect match for you!

Chartreux Cats make good companions at home and during long travels as well! You'll find that they can easily get along with the members of the family and even with other cats and dogs, which makes living with this cat breed a breeze.

Did we mention that Chartreux cats are also highly-reliable when it comes to rat patrol? You will surely be impressed with the accuracy of its pouncing and its perfect timing!

Delve into the world of this good-natured cat, and you might just find yourself thinking that a Chartreux Cat is the pet you need right now.

Table of Contents

Chapter One: Introduction to Chartreux Cat 1

Chapter Two: The Chartreux Cat Breed in a Nutshell 3

Origin 4

Chartreux Cat Breed Recognition around the World 6

Physical Traits 7

Behavioral Traits 9

Chapter Three: Frequently Asked Questions about Owning a
Chartreux Cat 11

What makes the Charteux cat breed a great pet? 12

What are the Pros and Cons of Owning a Chartreux Cat?
.... 13

Legal Requirements 20

Laws and Licensing of Cats in the United States 20

Laws and Licensing of Cats in the United Kingdom 22

Travelling With Your Pet 23

Chapter Four: Preparing a Warm Welcome for Your Cat 25

The Ideal Home for Cats 26

Environmental Enrichment 31

Helping your cat adjust to a new home 37

Introducing your new cat to other household pets 39

Cat-to-cat introduction 39

Cat-to-dog introduction..40

Living in a multi-cat home...41

Chapter Five: Breeding Chartreux Cats 43

Questions you should ask your cat breeder 44

Becoming a good cat breeder...46

Chapter Six: Home Equipment You'll Need for Chartreux

Cats..49

The Basic Needs of Chartreux cats.................................50

Food and Water Bowls...50

Kitty Litter 51

Bedding..53

Toys 53

Cat Furniture...53

Cat Enclosures..54

Why you should keep your Chartreux cat indoors...........56

Chapter Seven: Feeding Your Chartreux Cat......................59

The Basics of Cats' Nutritional Needs...............................60

Frequently asked questions about feeding a Chartreux cat

....62

Chapter Eight: Showing your Chartreux Cat........................67

The Chartreux Cat Breed Standard.....................................68

What you need to know about Cat Shows 71

Being a Spectator in Cat Shows 73

Entering a Cat Show with Your Pet Charteux 75

Classification of cats 76

Things to bring during the show day 77

Guidelines during the show day 77

Training Your Cat for a Show 80

Chapter Nine: Keeping Chartreux Cats Healthy 83

An Overview of the Chartreux Cat's health 85

Patellar Luxation 85

Obesity 89

Grooming a Chartreux cat 91

Training Your Chartreux cat 93

Should I spay or neuter my Chartreux cat? 94

Spaying and Neutering Costs 94

Chapter Ten: Care Sheet and Summary 97

Glossary of Cat Terms 109

Index 115

Photo Credits 119

References 121

Chapter One: Introduction to Chartreux Cat

Chartreux Cats are considered one of the oldest natural cat breed to ever exist. Although its exact origins are unknown, these cats are said to have been around since the 16th century, according to French Literature.

One of the first things you'll notice about the Chartreux is its unique, water-repellant coat, which could be a regal shade of Blue or Gray, while its eyes, a deep Orange. Chartreux cats could be one of the most elegant-looking felines you will see. This breed has a large, muscular built, but its legs are typically medium-short in length, and are fine-boned.

The Chartreux have always been great hunters. Don't be fooled by their calm demeanor, they are intelligent and move in a swift and well-calculated manner. They will never let unwelcome rodents roam around your house, that's for sure!

The fun in discovering more about the Chartreux doesn't stop there! You'll be surprised to know that contrary to its monotonous blue-gray coat, Chartreux cats are actually playful and they love interacting with their human friends. They tend to follow you around observe what you do, and show you utmost devotion, so remember to open to them not only your home, but also your heart.

I know what you're thinking: "Finally, here's a cat who likes receiving attention just as I like giving it!" You're right about that, although you'll have to be sensitive about the Chartreux's behavior for any signs of discomfort, because this is a breed that rarely makes noise. These felines are more likely to chirp than meow, which is why they made perfect companions for the Carthusian monks!

I think it's safe to say that you'll fall in love with this breed by the end of this guide, so read on, and we'll let you in on the best ways to keep them happy and healthy in your home!

Chapter Two: The Chartreux Cat Breed in a Nutshell

There is a lot to love about Chartreux Cats. On some days, this rare breed from France might wow you with its alertness and fast reflexes, and on other days, you may find its silence either comforting or confusing, but there's no questioning their loyalty to their human companions.

Chartreux Cats occasionally exhibit dog-like behavior like playing fetch and responding when their name is called. They are the type to enjoy watching other wildlife from the window, and chirp at the things they find interesting.

This chapter will tell you all about this beautiful breed's origins, where its vitality could have sprung from, and why they make an ideal pet for the household.

Origin

Could Chartreux Cats be just as mysterious as the color of their coat suggests? Well, they could be! You see, the exact origin of the Chartreux Cat Breed is unknown; however, there are three main beliefs as to how these lovely cats were discovered:

- Legend has it that the Chartreux's ancestors were feral mountain cats, and either crusaders or merchants were the ones who brought the Chartreux Cats to France from the Middle East.

- Another suggests that Monks of the Carthusian order bred these cats and made them their companions and protectors of Le Grande Chartreux Monastery's grain storage in southeastern France. Carthusian monks were known to be silent and solitary, that enthusiasts believed they may have imposed silence on Chartreux companions as well. Carthusian monks were also famous for theirCharteuseliquer, made from various herbs and flowers, thus, naming their feline friends Chartreux cats.

- It could also be possible that the breed's coat's woolly texture looked a lot like *la pile des Chartreux,* a type of Spanish wool popular in the early 18th century, and that's where they could've gotten their name.

Having originated in France,Chartreux cats were known as the country's national cat, albeit unofficially. French general, Charles de Gaulle owned one himself and named it "Gris Gris."

In 1558, a poem titled "VersFrançais sur la mort d'un petit chat" (French verse on a small kitten's death), was written by French poet Joachim du Bellay. The verse read:

"Here lies Belaud, my little gray cat,
Belaud, that was the most handsome perhaps
That nature ever made in cat's clothing.
This was Belaud, death to rats.
Belaud, to be sure his beauty was such
That he deserves to be immortal."

It was believed to be a remembrance of a Chartreux cat named Ballaud, who served very well as a rat hunter and a great companion.

The Chartreux also appeared in a portrait painted by French artist Jean-Baptiste Perronneau in 1747. It showed Magdaleine Pinceloup de la Grange, an aristocrat, holding a large cat with distinct features: gray fur and copper eyes.

Chartreux Cat Breed Recognition around the World

The breed was first imported to the United States by cat-lovers John and Helen Gamon. The two have read about the Chartreux in a book, and travelled all the way to Paris from La Jolla, California to purchase their dream cat, but Chartreux cats are so rare that they are said to be uncommon even in France where they originated!Finally, after three weeks of searching, they found Chartreux cats to take home from Madame Bastide's cattery. The Chartreuxthen made its debut in America in 1970, which makes it a relatively new breed in the U.S.

The Gamons then realized that there weren't any other registered Chartreuxes in Canada and the U.S. aside from theirs, so they took that as a good opportunity to import more Chartreux cats. It was only in 1987 when the Cat Fanciers' Association (CFA) gave the Chartreux full breed recognition.

The breed was almost eliminated in the early 1970's in Europe when FédérationInternationaleFéline (FIFe) joined the Chartreux with a British Shorthair, and then adopted the British Shorthair standard for both. This led to a protest by several French breeders, presenting papers to prove that the Chartreux is indeed a distinct breed.

Thankfully, in 1977, FIFe came up with a separate standard for both the Chartreux and British Shorthair. Just when there were only a few genuine Chartreux cats left, but the verdict came in just in time! The standards agreed upon since that year are still the ones being used today by the CFA and all North American cat associations.

Physical Traits

Chartreux cats in America tend to be purer bred than those you can find in Europe, this is due to some European breeders combining a Chartreux with a British Shorthair back in the 1970's. Want to know how to spot a genuine Chartreux cat? Take note of the breed standards below, set by none other than the Cat Fanciers' Association.

Head and facial features: Chartreux cats are well-loved for their "smile." As if their round head, short neck, and full cheeks don't make them adorable enough, the Chartreux's narrow, tapered muzzle makes it appear like it is always smiling. They also have a powerful-looking jaw, which sets them apart from other gray-colored breeds.

Adding to its cuteness, Chartreux cats usually have brilliant orange or copper eyes that are so expressive, you'd think they actually understand your conversations!

The Chartreux's nose, like its ears are medium-sized. Their ears stand erect high on their head, making them look alert at all times.

Body: Described widely as "a potato on toothpicks," the Chartreux indeed looks endearing with their well-muscled body, and a deep chest mounted on fine-boned, yet sturdy legs. They also have a moderately-long tail that's very responsive. Their feet are round and delicate you almost wouldn't believe it belongs rightfully to a cat this robust!

Female Chartreux cats are usually medium-sized, weighing 6 to 11 pounds, while males grow larger, between 10-16 pounds. Chartreux cats grow moderately tall, which makes them agile and less clumsy.

Coat: Chartreux cats are often mistaken for British Shorthair cats because of their similarities in their fur color. Although both breeds have blue or gray-colored coats, the Chartreux's coat is water-repellant and is noticeably woolly. They also have pretty dense undercoats that make the perfect protection from various elements. This particular physical trait justifies the belief that the early Chartreux cats were indeed born to hunt, patrolling the streets, farms, shops and homes in France in the previous centuries, keeping those places vermin-free.

The texture of the Chartreux's coat varies by age, sex, and environment. Females may have silkier and slightly thinner fur, while mature male Chartreux cats boast heavy coats.

By now, I'm sure you'd agree when we say that the Chartreux is quite an attractive breed!

Behavioral Traits

The Chartreux definitely falls on the 'quiet' side of the personality spectrum. Unlike other prominent breeds, Chartreux cats are generally silent—the only time you'd probably hear them vocalize their thoughts is when something greatly interests them, like the sight of a potential prey a.k.a. a toy, and you'd only be hearing them chirp and trill.

Although they rarely make noise, Chartreux cats are communicative and friendly. They aren't very demanding, but they would enjoy following you around, observing the things you do, and occasionally bumping their head on your feet as a sign of affection. Chartreux cats easily get along with family members of all ages because of their good nature. They make great companions at home and even on the road. You wouldn't have to worry about them disturbing your good night's sleep with incessant meowing as this breed hardly ever meows, but that never made them less adorable!

Chartreux cats aren't really the lazy type, but you'll have to keep them interested to keep them happy! You can expect them to be snuggled up comfortably beside you one minute, and then pouncing on its toys on the next. One way to keep your Chartreux cat entertained is by giving them puzzle toys that they can manipulate, but make sure you'll be prepared to give them treats, because this breed is also known to be highly intelligent!

At times, Chartreux cats may exhibit dog-like behavior like learning to play fetch and responding when its name is called! You might think it's silly, but you'll definitely fall in love with them. Just imagine all the fun moments you can have with a lovable Chartreux cat!

If you have dogs or other cats in the house and you're thinking of adding a Chartreux to the family, you'd be pleased to know that this breed adapts quickly and it surely wouldn't object their company as long as they are properly introduced to each other.

Chapter Three: Frequently Asked Questions about Owning a Chartreux Cat

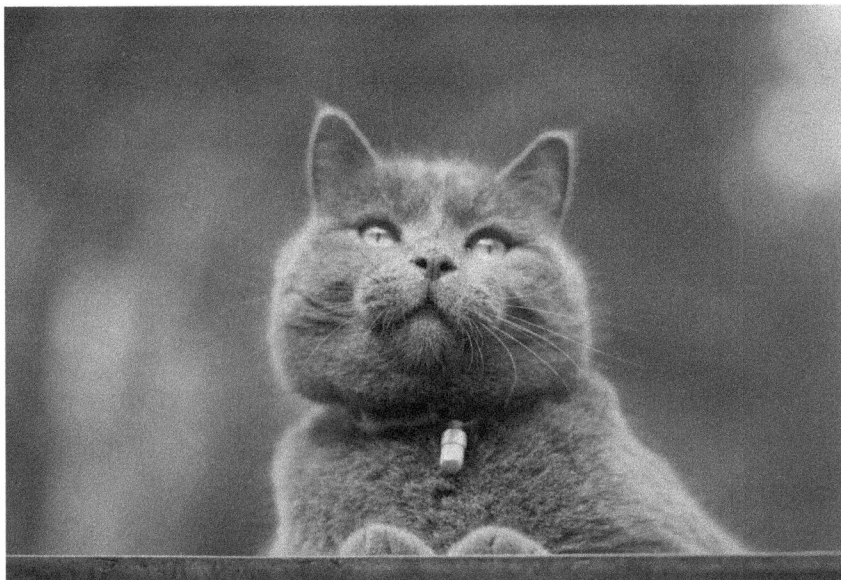

Pet ownership entails great responsibility. Just like any other human being, pets need attention, love, and care to live a normal, happy life.

Introducing a Chartreux cat to the family is no doubt, a great idea as Chartreux cats love being around humans, and can match the energy levels of playful kids. However, you'll need to know more than that to become an awesome owner to an equally awesome Chartreux cat. Luckily, this chapter will lay down all you need to know before bringing home this lovely gray cat.

What makes the Charteux cat breed a great pet?

General temperament:

- **Loyal but independent** –The Chartreux easily gets attached to its human companions, but their independence will particularly be observable when the Chartreux cats are around children. They will be very gentle, but they also are likely to step back and assess what's happening, so it will be best to keep an eye on toddlers during playtime with the Chartreux to make sure the cat isn't being mistreated or hurt.

- **Adaptable and friendly** –Chartreux cats have no problems sharing their home with other dogs or cats. They will definitely get along with your other pets as long as they are properly introduced.

- **Quiet but communicative** – Although you may find yourself living with a very silent cat, you can still expect to be showered with their affection and devotion. Chartreux cats are the type to follow you around from room to room to see how they can be involved in what you're doing, so remember to return the love by petting them generously and cradling them into your arms.

Because the Chartreux rarely express their emotions through meowing, owners must always be sensitive about their actions. Familiarize yourself with their behavior to avoid feeling clueless when they start acting differently, like showing signs of pain or discomfort.

Chartreux cats have a very sunny disposition, so make sure to treat them with kindess and patience, and they will reward you by being a friend for life.

What are the Pros and Cons of Owning a Chartreux Cat?

All cat lovers would agree that once in their life, they had wished there was a way to conjure the cat of their dreams—one that would complement every aspect of its owner's personality while looking like absolutely adorable according to its owner's taste. Although www.buildacat.com will probably never exist (not that we want it to!), there are numerous guides available to help you determine the best cat for your personality, your environment, your age, and other factors that need consideration on your part.

As for the Chartreux cat, you'd be glad to know that it is a fairly pleasant cat to bring home! Read carefully as we've gathered the most essential pros and cons you need to be aware of!

PROs

Companionship:

- Chartreux cats make great family cats.
- Easily gets along with other pets.
- Will instantly light up a room with its playfulness.
- Enjoys traveling by land.

Health:

- The Chartreux is known to be a healthy cat breed.
- Rarely have genetic defects.

Grooming:

- This breed only has few grooming requirements.
- Their short coat makes it easy to care for them.
- Your fingers alone already make a good comb for their coat! Brushing the Chartreux's coat once a week is ideal.
- Regular bathing is unnecessary for this breed, unless it is a show cat.

Attitude:

- Quiet
- Intelligent
- Affectionate
- Loves receiving attention
- Loyal

- Playful

CONs

Health:

- Chartreux cat owners must look out for tendencies of Patellar Luxation or a popping knee cap.
- May be prone to polycystic kidney disease and stones in the urinary tract. Encourage your cat to drink more water to avoid this health issue.
- Diet must be strictly controlled as this breed is thick and large. Overfeeding results to obesity that is bad for the Chartreux thin legs.

Shedding:

- Chartreux cats have a tendency to shed a couple of times a year, particularly during spring and fall.

Coat care:

- The Chartreux may develop a thick undercoat that may become extremely matted. Use a comb with medium or coarse teeth in the event of this.
- This breed's water-repellant coat makes it difficult to get it wet down to the skin when bathing.

Availability:

- The Chartreux is a very rare cat breed, so extensive research is required for you to find a reputable Chartreux cat breeder.
- Because they are rare, Chartreux cats are also a bit more expensive that other cat breeds.

Attitude:

- Although generally lively, Chartreux cats may be docile at times, choosing to take naps instead of playing. This is natural for them, so there's no need to worry when this happens.
- Their silence may make it difficult for owners to uncover their feelings, so be keen in observing your pet Chartreux's behavior or a change in it.

What is the proper pronunciation of the breed name?

Keep the letter "x" silent and pronounce it as "shar-TROO."

Should I worry about my Chartreux's diet?

Chartreux cats easily put on weight, so owners must be careful not to over feed them, especially if they are neutered. Some Chartreux cats may also be extremely sensitive to changes in their diet, so we highly recommend that you consult a veterinarian to know the best diet for your kitty.

Are Chartreux cats Hypoallergenic?

The Chartreux's thick undercoat tends to undergo heavy shedding on some seasons. The fur in their undercoat is short and can easily get caught in your eyes and nose. This breed may not be recommended for people with allergies.

Is the Chartreux cat blue or gray?

Generally, Chartreux cats are gray in color, but one can't help but notice that some Chartreux cat coats may look blue rather than gray, or vice versa. The CFA standards accept any Chartreux coat color in gray or blue shade from ash to slate. Some Chartreux cats have noticeable silver-brushed coat tips as well.

Why are Chartreux cats being confused with British Shorthair cats? How can I tell them apart?

The best explanation for this confusion would be their similar coat and eye colors. Both breeds come in gray-blue, but British Shorthair cats also come in other shades such as cream and brown. Both breeds' eyes are in copper or gold tones.

Although the two breeds both have chunky bodies, you can easily spot the Chartreux cat by looking at its legs; those of a Chartreux breed are more slender. Also, a Chartreux cat's coat is woolly to the touch while a British Shorthair's coat is single-coated and dense. You'll also notice that the position of the ears of these two breeds are different; the Chartreux cat's pointy ears are set high on their head, while the British Shortair's ear are far apart.

What is the average life span of Chartreux cats?

With proper love and care, Chartreux cats may live for 12-15 years or beyond that. Their maturity runs slow, only being noticeable at their 3rd year. Chartreux cats are greatly influenced by their environment and the attention being given to them; at times, you may feel as if you are taking care of an angsty teenager!

How much do Chartreux cats cost?

Since the Chartreux is a rare cat breed, breeders may charge you not lower than $500 up to $1,000 for a pet Chartreux. Prices may depend on whether you are looking for a Chartreux kitten or adult. If you intend to own a pet Chartreux for show, it is highly advisable that you research well and talk to different Chartreux cat breeders to know more about bloodlines before buying one.

Are Chartreux cats ideal for newbie cat owners?

Frankly speaking, taking care of a rare pure breed cat may not be for everybody. There would be quite a lot to deal with if you choose a Chartreux cat as your first pet as you will have to keep up with their love for giving and receiving attention, control their diet, observe them closely and familiarize yourself with their silence and behavior, and make sure that their lovely coat does not end up matting. Indeed, it may seem like a lot of work for a newbie cat owner, but if you think that this adorable breed is a perfect match for you, find a trusted breeder, and live happily ever after with a pet Chartreux!

Is there a traditional naming system for the Chartreux cat breed?

Yes, there is. Chartreux cat owners are accustomed to using the French naming system for this breed wherein the year the kitten was born determines the first letter of its name. This tradition follows a 20-year cycle and uses letters in the alphabet excluding K, Q, W, X, Y, and Z. Don't you think it would be nice to follow the tradition? Take note of this when you have your pet Chartreux registered.

Legal Requirements

Cats are becoming a staple member of households and even private institutions all over the world, which make the presence of laws governing cat ownership essential.

Ultimately, laws are geared towards protecting pets from abuse and neglect as well as protecting the community from animals that may become threatening to the public.

As responsible pet owners, it is our duty to be fully informed about them and uphold them. By doing so, we are contributing to a better community not only for our feline friends, but also for ourselves, so we've rounded up the legal requirements you'll need to accomplish upon acquiring a Chartreux cat in America and the United Kingdom.

Laws and Licensing of Cats in the United States

Unlike dog owners, cat owners are not required to obtain a license for their cats across all states in the U.S., except in Rhode Island, where it is mandated. However, there are some municipal ordinances that may require proof of vaccination and identification, particularly in Alabama, where owners are required to have their cat or dog vaccinated yearly to make sure that all pets, owners, and civilians are protected from rabies. This is actually a good measure in the event of cat bites and scratches. Remember, cats can be infected with rabies, too, so if you haven't yet, bring your pet to a vet and ask to be scheduled for vaccination as soon as possible.

Cats are not required to wear collars in the U.S. as it is believed to go against their nature. It is, however, good for cats get used to wearing collars for reasons other than looking extra cute:

- **Easy identification.** In the event that your cat accidentally gets out the gate and gets lost, having the owner's contact details on the collar makes is easier for concerned citizens to help out.

- **It can serve as an alert for cats with medical conditions.** Leaving your cat in a pet inn while you're away on a trip? Then it is highly advisable to have their collar inscribed with any medical conditions they have to ensure that your cat will be properly fed and cared for. Same goes for when your cat goes missing; people who found it would immediately know that the cat needs special medical attention.

Reminder: To make sure that your cat's collar won't interfere with its movements or cause injuries, always check if it is properly secured on the neck. If you can slip two fingers between the collar and the kitty's neck, then it's all good! A collar that's too tight might cause irritation, while having it too loose might cause it to get snagged on objects.

For further information regarding licensing requirements and ordinances in your area, give your local government a call or simply look up their website, and check if there are downloadable forms for cat licensing. Once accomplished, mail it to the town hall or hand it over personally. Some states charge an average of $10.00 for regular citizens and $5.00 for senior citizens. The cost may vary across the states.

Laws and Licensing of Cats in the United Kingdom

Would you believe that Westminster is home to several cats who serve as mouse hunters? The U.K. definitely loves their feline friends so much that earlier this year, the government pledged to develop more laws to protect kittens from exploitation. This was after discovering that some kittens are being bred in poor conditions and are taken away from their mothers too soon. The new law states that license exemptions for people who repeatedly sell kittens that are bred from non-pedigree cats will be removed, and there will be stricter conditions for breeder licenses to be approved.

Since the U.K. has successfully eliminated Rabies in 1922, your cat may be required to undergo a quarantine period as a strict safety measure.

Travelling With Your Pet

The customs require, pet owners to indicate animals travelling with them in their declaration documents. Keep in mind that pets undergo the same procedures as baggage. You can immediately pick up your pet along with your baggage at the baggage claim if there are no quarantine requirements at your destination.

In the U.S., various states may impose their own regulations on interstate animal transportation, so it will be best to get in touch with the local government of the municipality you're planning to head to first before traveling. On the other hand, the U.K. requires special permits to be able to take your pet cat to or from the country.

Seek advice from your government office regarding the accomplishment of this special permit.

Traveling can be quite stressful for cats, as they are very sensitive about sound, temperature, and movement. It is important to consult a veterinarian before traveling to ensure that you will have all you need to keep them safe and healthy.

Chapter Four: Preparing a Warm Welcome for Your Cat

Waiting for a pet cat's arrival at home is one of the best feelings in the world. It's kind of like preparing for the arrival of a baby, only this one has fur, a tail, and walks on all fours. Whatever the size of your home is, you will definitely need to ensure that it is "Cat-proof" and an ideal place for your feline friend to thrive.

One thing that keeps a cat happy is knowing that it has a safe and comfortable home. Sometimes, though, a cat's curious nature gets it into trouble, creating a hassle both for you and himself. Older cats are less likely to be mischievous, while kittens are trickier to handle!

For sure you've seen tons of entertaining videos all over social media showing a tiny cat comfortably sleeping on a miniature bed tailor-made for it. Although it looks absolutely adorable, kittens will need more than just cozy sleeping furniture to grow healthy and strong. The surrounding environment greatly impacts a cat's overall health and behavior, which is why the U.S. and U.K. governments have given some reminders and recommendations regarding the housing of cats, specifically the amount of space, the furniture, interaction with other pets and with humans, and environmental enrichment including toys and other sensory stimulants. At first, these may seem a bit intimidating, but you surely won't regret abiding these in the long run!

This chapter will teach you tips and tricks to ensure that your home is ready for the arrival (and possibly, the reign) of the Chartreux cat.

The Ideal Home for Cats

According to research, cats are fairly comfortable living on their own. Unlike dogs, who tend to be very social and enjoy being in packs, cats would rather keep a distance to avoid social conflicts. That being said, here are some do's and don'ts's to bear in mind:

- **DO make sure that there will be hiding spots** where the cat can seek refuge and be out of sight at times when it feels stressed or uncomfortable with interactions.

- **DO make litter trays, water bowl, and food bowls easily accessible** for the Chartreux cat. In case you have more than one pet at home, give each pet their own bowls with sufficient supply of food to avoid monopolization. One of the most common conflicts among cats is guarding their resources from each other, but this may be avoided with proper allocation of their needs.

- **DO maximize vertical space** by incorporating elevated and vertical structures inside your house, such as:
  o Shelves
  o Slanted walkways
  o Climbing poles
  o Little hammocks
  o Steps
  o Resting boxes
  o Platforms
  o Cat trees

You don't need all of the things mentioned above, but having at least some of these in your house is highly essential when living with a cat. Felines prefer to spend more time in high places, and having them navigate through these structures will surely be a good exercise and entertainment for them (and for you as well, of course!).

- **DO keep containers closed at all times.** Kittens are naturally curious and are more likely to climb whatever structures they can. It is a must to keep water containers, garbage cans, and washers & dryers closed at all times as cats can get trapped inside when they fall. Also bear in mind that an open toilet bowl could attract thirsty kittens and may cause drowning, so protect your feline friends by keeping those lids closed.

- **DO provide comfortable bedding** in ideal resting areas. Cats enjoy resting in dry and warm areas, usually in corners where they feel more secure. Try to get creative and make cat beds from soft materials such as polyester fleece cloth, so you wouldn't need to spend much on new beds. Studies show that cats who sleep on soft surfaces tend to rest longer than those who sleep on hard surfaces. You extra effort will go a long way for your Chartreux cat!

- **DON'T encourage your cat to nap near hot surfaces like stoves or fireplaces.** Although they enjoy resting in warm areas, the fireplace and kitchen top are absolutely not safe places for rest. Gently wake up your cat and move it to a safer spot to remind them that these are not the correct places for napping.

- **DO allot one litter tray for 1-2 cats only.** This is the ideal allocation if you have several cats at home to ensure good toilet behavior. Remember that cleaning the litter box at least once per day is a must because some cats won't use a tray that's been soiled. You'll find a variety of cat litter in the groceries, and it may take some experimenting to know which type is the most ideal for your cat. Also keep in mind that the locations of the litter box and feeding bowls must be at least 0.50 meters apart and not be interchanged to prevent confusion.

- **DON'T leave hazardous and poisonous chemicals exposed.** Cats are curious and playful in nature. They will tinker with almost every object they come across with, and you wouldn't want you cat suddenly knocking over that bottle of bleach or detergent, or worse, accessing roach and rodent killers. Keep all dangerous substances secured in cabinets with locks. That way, both humans and felines will both be safe from these!

- **DO buy your Chartreux cat some toys to keep it busy.** Chartreux cats are known for their intelligence. They easily learn how to open doors, press buttons, and so much more that could get them into trouble!

Giving your cat some toys would keep it busy and entertained. Chartreux cats usually like fake mouse toys that they can chase around and pounce on. Puzzle toys are also ideal for them as they like figuring out how small objects work.

- **DON'T leave cords and strings dangling.** Both adult cats and kittens love chewing and playing with things they can reach or find on the ground. The problem is, getting badly entangled in these wires could cause choking. Rid your house of small, scattered items such as:
    - Rubber bands
    - Hair ties
    - Cable ties
    - Ribbons
    - Plastic bags
    - Rubber erasers
    - Sewing supplies such as thread and yarn
    - Small, hard toys you can find in board games
    - Doll accessories

- **DO tape and secure electrical wiring properly.** Kittens may think wires are fun to play with, but one wrong bite on this and they'll end up getting badly hurt or electrocuted, and may even cause electrical problems in your home. Avoid problems by checking the house for loose wirings before bringing in a new pet.

- **DON'T keep toxic plants at home.** Not all plants can be used as catnip, some turns out to be harmful to cats. The most common toxic houseplants are lilies, poinsettia Philodendron, and mistletoe. While garden plants that you should keep your cat away from are daffodils and azaleas. You can find an extensive list of toxic and non-toxic plants on the website of the American Society for the Prevention of Cruelty to Animals (ASPCA).

Environmental Enrichment

Once you've got the furniture ready for the Chartreux's arrival, it's now time to know how you can enhance the Chartreux cat's quality of life under your watch. Having an ideal house arrangement for pet cats is only the tip of the iceberg—as an owner, you'll need to plan on your enrichment activities for them, too!

Like humans, pets can get easily bored as well. We can't expect them to nap forever! Playtimes commonly happen after their naps, and this is a good time to stimulate their brain through interaction and physical activities.

Ellis (2009) states some goals of environmental enrichment: Ellis S (2009). Environmental enrichment: Practical strategies for improving feline welfare. *Journal of Feline Medicine and Surgery*, 11, 901-912.

- o To lessen the occurrences of abnormal behavior in cats.
- o Increase the chances of your cat using its environment in a positive way such as learning to enjoy himself with the use of the items he finds around him.
- o Increase the occurrences of normal behavioral patterns, as you may notice that cats are somewhat routinary.
- o Helping cats learn to cope with challenges in a more natural way.

Here are some tips to achieve an enriched environment for cats at home:

- **Stimulate their senses.** Set a little hammock or platform for your cat by the window to excite their eyes. Chartreux cats enjoy looking out windows and observing other people and animals. If you're lucky, you could hear them chirp and trill at the birds they'll see! Laser pointers may seem like a good idea, but Ellis warns that these may cause frustration in some cats, as they aren't able to interactwith the stimuli. You can also try letting your Chartreux cat explore your garden, but only if you are there to watch over it. You wouldn't want to chase them through the neighborhood, so make sure that your gates are closed and never let your Chartreux cat out of your sight.

- If you're ever tried listening to classical music, you'd know how effective it can be as a stress reliever. Some say that it has the same effects on cats and other animals. Although it hasn't been proven, there's no harm in playing soothing music for your Chartreux cat when you see it being hyper active or agitated. Certain types of sounds stimulate their auditory senses, which are called species-appropriate music. It is highly likely for cats to enjoy "music" that mimic the rhythm and tonal qualities of purrs. Well, who doesn't like the sound of cats purring anyway?

- In a study published in the Applied Animal Behavioral Sciences Journal in 2015, researchers explained that Feline-appropriate music have a pulse similar to purring 1,380 beats per minute. You'd probably find "Cat Music" playlists in some popular streaming platforms so go ahead and test these out on your pet Chartreux and carefully observe how it reacts. Just a gentle warning, mellow music intended to help your cat sleep might have the same effect on you!

- The type of music we usually like is definitely not the type they enjoy, so be sensitive to your pets before deciding to blast music from your speakers. It hasn't been determined yet whether cats prefer high-pitched or low-pitched sounds, but in general, extremely loud noise could be harmful to your cat.

- Olfactory stimulation should also be on your priority as cats are born with a highly-developed sense of smell. If you can observe, cats immediately react to certain smells; they get easily attracted by the scent of deliciously-cooked food, and they instantly back away from people, food, or objects whose scent they don't like or recognize. You can help enhance their sense of smell by providing posts or surfaces for scratching. This is especially helpful when you have more than one cat at home as cats communicate via their scent glands. Remember the time you saw your cat rubbing its head on a scratching post? It is an act of leaving their scent behind for other cats to recognize.

- Some cats also react to Nepeta Cataria, a.k.a Catnip. Nepetalactone is a chemical compound found in this dried herb's leaves and stem. When sniffed, it triggers the cat's pheromones, causing it to be hyperactive for a few minutes. You may see your cat suddenly flip or roll around as a reaction to sniffing Catnip, but don't worry! Catnip is absolutely safe for cats, but feeding them too much of this may cause diarrhea or vomiting. To avoid habituation, it's recommended that you don't give Catnip more than once every two to three weeks. Catnip is readily available in pet supplies stores, along with toys stuffed with it.

- **Incorporate natural feeding methods every once in a while.** Meal time is one, if not, a cat's most loved daily activity. Full and satisfied cats are happy cats; they sleep more soundly and behave better when they are not deprived of a good meal.

  Since the Chartreux are natural hunters, letting them perform natural feeding behaviors could greatly stimulate their appetite and even their brain functions. In the wild, cats hunt often and they end up eating 10 small meals daily. You can have your pet Chartreux experience experience stalking or "hunting" for their by using food puzzle toys where your cat has to figure out how to work the object in order to get its food. The best examples of these are:

  o **Treat balls –** The cat has to roll the ball, commonly known as an egg-sercizer, until cat food falls from the tiny holes all over the ball. You can make one at home by cutting holes on small containers, water bottles, or even toilet paper roles, and then, putting dry food inside it. Your cat will surely be intrigued by the sound the treats make when it moves the container. Later on, it'll start smelling the treats inside and the rest is history!

- o **Foraging feeders** – This type of food puzzle will not only allow cats to experience natural feeding behaviors, it can also help prevent cats from over indulging that leads to obesity. It mimics the experience of scooping out food from small, difficult spaces, which cats in the wild usually do.

- o **Play circuit boards** – This type of food puzzle toy was initially created for animals kept in zoos or in laboratories for observation. Cats simply manipulate objects in the circuit board in order to get their food. You can either buy ready-made boards or make one yourself. Check out tutorials online and create the best one for your cat that includes their favorite toys.

Each cat is unique and special in its own way, and sometimes they can get unpredictable. By doing your part as a Charteux cat owner, you are eliminating possible causes of behavior problems for house cats, such as frustration, boredom, and stress. Not many cat owners know how important it is to stimulate cats mentally and physically, and so they, too, become problematic when their pet cat starts destroying furniture, meowing uncontrollably at night, being aggressive, or worse, getting sick. These can be avoided by being aware of your cat's need to express their natural behaviors. If you succeed in creating an enriched environment for them, you will be rewarded with a peaceful and well-behaved cat.

Helping your cat adjust to a new home

Bringing home a new pet could be a really special experience for humans, but for cats, and other animals as well, it can be quite frightening. For you to be able to help them feel secure and ease their tension, you must first understand why cats are scared when being rehomed. Cats dislike change; for them, a new home means entering new territory, meeting new possible enemies, and encountering new challenges they are not all too familiar with.

On the ride home, make sure that your Chartreux cat is inside a carrier to that it feels safer. Being inside moving vehicles may traumatize your cat and cause it much stress that it would start to pant. Panting is a sure sign of anxiety and excessive body heating, so help your cat by keeping it safe inside a well-ventilated cat carrier.

Chapter Four: Preparing a Warm Welcome for Your Cat

Upon arriving home, it is advised that you let your cat settle into a small room that he can call his early territory or "home base." Do not force the cat out of the carrier, instead, keep it open and let the cat decide when it is comfortable enough to explore the room. You can have your cat stay in the room for several days so that he gets used to the smells, the sounds, and the sights. Put everything the cat needs in this room, including water and food bowls, litter tray, a few toys to keep him busy, and a comfortable bedding.

You may visit the cat often to see if it is doing fine, but don't stress it out by giving it forced attention or by bringing in new people to the room to pet or play with the cat. Also see to it that your kids don't frighten the cat by entering their haven uninvited. Chartreux cats are known to easily adapt to its environment, but letting them get used to their new home and new human companions at their own pace will work wonders on your relationship with them.

The amount of time a cat will finally feel comfortable in its new home varies according to its past experiences and personality. Giving a cat ample time to adjust to a new home will be beneficial both for you and your pet, and you will be spared fear-induced cat-spraying or house-soiling, uncontrollable meows, violence, mistrust, and hiding,

Introducing your new cat to other household pets

One thing more difficult than introducing a new cat to humans is introducing it to other pets because it's not easy controlling animal behavior, much less, decoding their thoughts and understanding what they're trying to say!

You can expect that one pet of yours will always try to dominate your new cat, as animals are territorial in nature. Being wise about their "getting-to-know" period is highly important, so extend your patience and trust the process.

Cat-to-cat introduction

An older cat is likely to accept another adult cat much easier than it is to like new kittens at once. It will be best to separate the resident cats from the new cat upon arrival, so that you can manage their initial encounter. If you have more than one resident cat at home, introduce them to the new cat individually.

It's not necessary to have the cats spend time together immediately. Keep the cat in its temporary room until it feels confident enough to roam around. Keep an eye out for when your cats see each other for the first time. Make sure that they keep a distance to prevent aggression, as first impressions indeed last.

If there will be no signs of hostility among the cats in the coming days, you may now let them spend time together without a worry.

Cat-to-dog introduction

Because dogs are larger than cats, meeting a resident dog may be a scary experience for your new cat. Luckily for you, Chartreux cats have a pleasant attitude, therefore, making them dog-friendly. It is highly advisable that you keep your dog confined or in a leash upon the arrival of the new cat. Make sure that the cat's initial base is not accessible to the dog to prevent it from cornering of chasing the cat, even if it only wants to play. Do not let your dog frighten the cat by showing signs of aggression or intimidating the cat by barking, as this can be stressful for a Chartreux cat.

Give your cat and dog enough time to get to know each other by not forcing interaction. Do not leave them alone together unsupervised if you are not sure yet whether they like each other or not. Hopefully, after a few weeks, you'll see them peacefully hanging around the house and being each other's new best friend.

Living in a multi-cat home

You probably enjoyed the company of one cat so much that you are considering bringing home another one. To set your expectations, here are some pros and cons of living with multiple cats at home.

PROs	CONs
Decreased signs of behavior problems. Solitary cats are more likely to get frustrated when being left home alone because of boredom and loneliness, while cats in pairs or in groups have each other to play with and keep them company.	**More paws could mean more trouble.** A cat with a buddy may now be able to pull off more mischief than it has when it was alone. Be sure to cat-proof furniture and other important appliances. Keep their food supply locked away to prevent food wasting and playing.
Grooming made easier. Cats enjoy helping each other clean themselves. Expect those hard-to-reach places to be cleaned by no other than their grooming buddy!	**It is time-consuming.** Multiple cats in the house entails more litter trays, food bowls, and water bowls clean. It also means clipping more nails, brushing more coats, and having to clean up

	more fur from the house.
Happier cats = happier home. Seeing cats cuddled up is truly something special. You may find that cats with company are less likely to be shy or frightened. They become more confident knowing that they have a buddy for life they can count on.	**Expenses are doubled.** The American Society for the Prevention of Cruelty to Animals (ASPCA) warns that you could spend $1,035 per year for basic cat needs. On top of food and litter expenses, veterinary visits and grooming costs could double up for you as well.

These are just some of the most basic things to consider before deciding to get a new cat or bringing multiple cats home. Assess your financial situation, space, current family life carefully before wanting to take care of more furry friends.

Chapter Five: Breeding Chartreux Cats

Chartreux cats are one of the oldest and rarest cat breeds, which makes owning one something you can definitely be proud of. Owning one adorable cat could have you feeling that you want to take care of more. Cat owners usually get inspired to breed cats after visiting cat shows, where they find cute kittens, or after hearing positive stories from other cat breeders. But before you decide to start breeding Chartreux cats for sale, for show, or for additional companions in your home, you'll have to be prepared to face struggles involving finances, emotions, and time management. This chapter answers the questions you have regarding breeding Chartreux cats, and how you can spot reputable breeders yourself.

Questions you should ask your cat breeder

Before becoming a cat breeder yourself, you are going to have to find reputable cat breeders whom you can buy your first Chartreux cat from. There are a lot of people who claim to be "trusted" breeders, but end up being otherwise. In order to spot a reputable breeder, here are some questions you can ask them:

Do they have a breeders' contract?

A written agreement is important in this given situation for both parties to be protected in the presence of legal problems.

Do the kitten's parents have certifications?

A good cat breeder will be able to support their claims with documents and certifications. Do not trust breeders who say that their kittens have no family history of medical conditions. That, and those who do not give health guarantees must not be chosen as your breeder.

Does the breeder belong to any breeders' association or club?

If so, ask for reviews or references before buying from this breeder.

Does the breeder join cat shows?

Being exposed to cat shows could give breeders more information about the different cat breeds they offer. Moreover, if a breeder has had some champion cats, it could be a good sign of high-quality cats. Do note, though, that if a breeder seems to give importance to collecting trophies rather than the cats themselves, it could be a red flag.

How many cats do you raise per year?

If a breeder raises a large number of kittens per year, there is a chance of having epidemics run through their cattery. If you see a large number of male cats on their list of breeding cats, then you should also be cautious as to how they are able to maintain and properly care for many cats.

What you need to know about kitten mills and kitten farms

First thing's first: avoid buying from kitten mills. These owners are bad breeders in a nutshell, and they do not care about the welfare of the cats and kittens. In kitten mills, the cats live in harsh conditions, such as sharing as sharing space with too many cats, not getting enough medical attention, and living in their own waste.

Owners of kitten mills often do not show any concern for their cats' health, and they only want to keep selling cats for profit.

Kitten mills will only cease to exist once people stop buying from them, but the problem is, a lot of people do not know how to spot them. If you notice that someone claiming to be a breeder know less about the breed they raise, does not show any health guarantees, and won't allow you to see kitten's parents, do not push through with the rehoming or adoption. If you want to become a cat breeder yourself, support only the good breeders and avoid transactions with owners of kitten mills, kitten farms, backyard breeders, and hoarders.

Becoming a good cat breeder

There could be many reasons as to why a cat owner decides to become a breeder. Having lots of kittens at home could mean more cute playmates and positive energy, and making this your hobby or passion could open doors for you as a cat owner and breeder. However before you jump in to Chartreux cat breeding, here are some questions you should ask yourself:

Do you have extra time to breed cats?

Cat breeding will definitely take much of your time. If you have a family to take care of and a day job to focus on, determine whether the spare time you have will be enough to be a responsible cat breeder. Remember, more cats equals more litter boxes to clean, more vet visits, more claws to trim, and so on.

Are you financially-ready to become a breeder?

You may think that cat breeding will make you a millionaire, but that is not the case. Cat breeding entails having to invest in cats with breeding rights, their medical bills when giving birth, excellent grooming, and setting up a decent space.

Are you willing to learn more to become an expert on Chartreux cats?

You will have to devote time to attending cat shows and conferences, researching, and communicating with breeder organizations in order to learn more about your chosen breed. In order to become a credible cat breeder, you need to know as much information as you can about your chosen cat breed.

Can you handle possible emotional tolls that cat breeding can give you?

Common issues for cat breeders involve seeing kittens be born dead, watching their beloved cat die due to complications while giving birth, and the general stress of caring for multiple cats. More concerns arise as you continue on with breeding cats. You really must be mentally tough enough to become a cat breeder and to face the challenges that come along with it.

Although cat breeding may seem discouraging and limiting, nothing can compare to the joy of successful births and snuggling with more sweet Chartreux kittens. Seek advice from seasoned breeders for some motivation.

Chapter Six: Home Equipment You'll Need for Chartreux Cats

Any type of pet you intend to keep will definitely cost you additional expenses. However, the price to pay is usually no match for the joy that owning a pet gives any household. Chartreux cats are generally low maintenance, but that doesn't mean you can maintain them without extra effort.

As a responsible pet owner, it is your task to know the ideal environment for this breed to keep them feeling happy and secure in your home. Knowing the general temperament of this breed in the previous chapters help a lot in planning out for their needs and preferences to make sure they can co-exist with you comfortably in your own home.

Chapter four gives you a breakdown of all that you need to prepare for your pet Chartreux such as enclosures, basic needs, accessories, and your possible, average expenses.

The Basic Needs of Chartreux cats

Like us humans, cats have their own needs, too, including a place to sleep, bowls to eat in, and entertainment. Preparing these before their arrival will save you much time and effort. It will also allow you to find the best ones for them with your budget.

Food and Water Bowls

If you are bringing home a kitten, the best type of bowls to choose are the shallow ones to allow easy access to their food and water.

There are many types of bowls to choose from, and plastic is the most popular. However, this material is known to retain smells that the cat may find foul and may discourage them from finishing their food. In some cases, cats that are allergic to plastic end up having a type of cat acne on their chin.

So far, the most recommended type of food bowl is stainless steel because it is sturdy and generally harmless for cats. Steel bowls are often dishwasher safe, which could help busy owners save time. Make sure to keep the food bowls clean and rinse them regularly to prevent the build-up of bacteria. Depending on the quality ad type, you can spend as low as $3 for a single bowl, or as low as $6 for a set of 2.

Kitty Litter

Cats tend to do their potty business in the same areas, unlike dogs that need to be walked until they find an ideal area. To take advantage of this, you'll need to get your cat a litter box. There a lot of types if litter boxes depending on your budget and your preferences. There is even an automated poop handler that could do the dirty work for you. Depending on your cat's personality, you can either choose a hooded litter box from privacy or a plain plastic tray for those who don't enjoy feeling boxed.

As for the litter, you may have to experiment and observe what your cat prefers. Here are the types of cat litter to consider:

- Clumping clay
- Non-clumping clay
- Grass
- Wheat
- Silica gel crystals
- Crushed Walnut shells
- Recycled paper
- Corn-based litter

The most common type of litter available in the groceries are clumping-cat litter. This type is highly-absorbent, making it easy to clean, although it tends to be a bit dusty. Prices of cat litter usually start at $14.

Cat Litter Tray Maintenance

- Fill the litter box up to 2-3 inches so that the cat can dig through it and learn to cover its waste.
- Scoop out the waste at least 2-3 times daily. Some cats would not use a soiled litter box, so to prevent them from doing their business elsewhere, keep their tray clean.
- Dispose the soiled litter properly by bagging it. Avoid using this as fertilizer as it will surely attract other cats, flies, and insects. Do not flush the litter to prevent drainage problems.

Bedding

Cats will absolutely like anything soft. You may opt for a pillow or a cat bed. Consider the size of your cat when buying bedding; a bed too large might leave the cat feeling unsettled, and a bed too small will ultimately be uncomfortable.

Since Chartreux cats are affectionate creatures, you can also expect your cat to snuggle beside you on your own bed. Hopefully, that wouldn't be a problem for you!

Toys

Stock up on toys so that you and your family can bond with your pet Chartreux. Playtime is important for a kitten's development and it can be therapeutic for us humans, too! Basically, you can buy any type of cat toy you wish, just remember to avoid buying those with parts than can cause choking or strangling. There are a lot of cheap cat toys in the stores and online, so you don't have to worry about spending much on them.

Cat Furniture

Scratch posts/pads, cat condos, and cat trees are an ideal part of your home of you are living with a cat. These structures allow there to express their natural behaviors such as leaving marks on their territory and climbing. Costs depend on the type you want, but cat furniture prices usually start at around $20.

Cat Enclosures

Cat enclosures or "cat patios" are structures that provide protection for your cat outdoors. This is the perfect solution for your cat to enjoy the sights and sounds of the world outside while keeping it safe. If you're having second thoughts about allowing your cat outdoors, building a cat enclosure will provide the environmental enrichment that it needs.

Here are some benefits of having a cat enclosure, as told by Catio Spaces, a known cat enclosure builder:

- Reduction of veterinary bills due to contracted illnesses and injuries from the outdoors.
- Giving your cat a healthier lifestyle by being able to sunbathe, bird watching, additional exercise, and fresh air intake.
- Lessening indoor odors by providing another litter box in the enclosure.
- Helping reduce the free-roaming cat population in the neighborhood.

Of course, setting up an enclosure entails your time, effort, and additional costs. You can either hire a builder and designer, or you can go the extra mile and do it yourself.

Organic Authority shared an easy DIY cat enclosure project that will cost you less than $200. Here's how you could start planning for it:

o **Choose an ideal location.** Find a spot that you cat/s can easily access like a door, an existing window or a patio where you can build a "cat door." Also make sure that the location you' choose won't too warm, as exposure to direct sunlight during the hottest periods of the day could be harmful to your cats.

o **Accessibility to humans.** You'll need to be able to access the enclosure as well for cleaning and maintenance.

o **Consider the age of your cat.** This will help you decide what type of furniture you'll need to install in the enclosure. Ramps are ideal for older cats.

o **Evaluate your budget.** Bigger or more elaborate enclosures could look nice, but keep in mind that you'll be having other expenses for food, grooming and vet visits—you wouldn't want to blow your budget on an enclosure.

Once you're sure of what you want for your Chartreux's enclosure, you may now check available supplies with your local hardware store and start building. Some of the basic things you'll need are galvanized wire, lumber for framing, and wire mesh or polycarbonate panels for roofing options.

Why you should keep your Chartreux cat indoors

You may think that your cat longs to be let outside to interact with other cats and enjoy the outdoors, but for rare breeds like the Chartreux, it is strongly advised not to let them outside unsupervised. There are a lot of risks that come along with allowing them outdoors, such as:

- Getting lost and being seen by Animal Control.
- Fighting with other cats
- Being chased by dogs or other larger animals
- Contracting fleas, ticks, and other harmful parasites.
- Catching infections from stray cats and dogs
- Getting hit by vehicles
- Getting poisoned by substances like rat bait
- Putting the lives of human companions in danger by contracting parasites harmful for humans.

Instead of letting your pet cat outside, you can create a haven for them inside your house instead. Like all cats, the Chartreux enjoys living in a home where it has enough spaces for hiding in case it senses trouble or discomfort. Being hunters by nature, it is ideal for Chartreux cats to have platforms they could jump on, stairs they could travel, and even a nice place to sit on by the window. You could also put a bird bath near the window as seeing birds may keep your cat entertained.

Chapter Seven: Feeding Your Chartreux Cat

Maintaining proper nutrition for your pet Chartreux is one of the most important yet complex aspects of cat ownership. Oftentimes, owners don't understand how much diet affects a cat's behavior, health, and even longevity, and so they end up neglecting proper feeding schedules and amounts of intake.

Since the Chartreux is a naturally muscular and full-bodied cat, owners must make sure that their food intake is controlled to avoid obesity. Proper nutrition for this breed is essential for their overall health and heart development.

The Chartreux is typically not a picky eater, but there are certain types of food that can be good and bad for them. This section will cover the proper nutrition that Chartreux cats needs the best feeding practices you can to keep your pet Chartreux in its optimal health.

The Basics of Cats' Nutritional Needs

Similar to us humans, out feline companions also need a healthy diet to thrive. Feeding your Chartreux cat the wrong food could lead to a health disaster, so it is important to know the best diet for them before filling up their stomach.

In a nutshell, cats need the following nutrients to grow healthy:

Minerals – Minerals are involved in most of a cat's physiological reactions like pH balance, enzyme formulation, oxygen transportation, and nutrient utilization. The following minerals are needed by cats on a daily basis: chloride, chromium, copper, calcium, cobalt, iodine, iron, zinc, magnesium, manganese, and potassium.

Knowing the proper amount needed by your pet is best determined by your veterinarian. If you've already bought some cat food but are not sure if it is good for your cat, bring the cat food to your vet to have its nutritional values assessed.

Protein – Cats need a great amount of protein in their body. The Chartreux cat can get a good supply of this from meat, as plant sources do not supply Taurine, an essential amino acid that cats need. Taurine deficiency in cats can lead to a declining health, or worse, death, so make sure to include protein-rich food in their diet.

Vitamins – Vitamins are important to our pets as it is for us humans. Cats need these nutrients for good metabolism, and for normal growth and bodily functions. The Chartreux cat needs a great supply Vitamin A which can be found in animal meat. Plant-sourced vitamins such as beta-carotene can't be utilized by the cat's body.

Water – Cats have low levels of thirst because they can fulfill much of their water requirements by eating fresh, raw food. This is why cats that eat dry food often have more health issues than those who eat wet cat food. Cats that lack water in their body end up getting dehydrated and usually have urine that is too concentrated.

Always prepare fresh and clean drinking water for your Chartreux cat. If you feel that they are not drinking enough, you can get cat drinking fountains that mimic the experience of drinking from running water, which a Chartreux may prefer as well.

Fatty Acids – Essential Fatty Acids are another example of nutrients that cats can't convert from plant sources, which again justifies why a cat's diet needs to be composed of meat. These nutrients are involved with metabolism functions and cell integrity in a cat's body. Another fatty acid that cats need is the Gamma-linolenic acid, which improves the feline skin and coat.

In addition to the essential nutrients mentioned above, cats also produce antioxidants and enzymes within their body. These help protect the body from free radicals that can damage the cells. Antioxidants and enzymes can be found in healthy food sources for cats.

Frequently asked questions about feeding a Chartreux cat
Which types of food are toxic to cats?

While it's tempting to share your food with your pet Chartreux, do take note of the following human food that is toxic to them:

- Chocolates and drinks with caffeine
- Dairy products and milk
- Garlic and onion
- Raw dough
- Alcohol
- Raisins and grapes

Another food that you should skip giving your cat is Dog food. Although this isn't toxic to them, cats need a higher level of Taurine, Vitamin A, protein, and arachidonic acid, which are of low levels in dog food.

Do kittens and adult cats have the same food requirements?

You'd be surprised to know that kittens need more food for development than adult cats. Dr. Francis Kallfelz, DVM, Ph, D., from the American College of Veterinary Medicine states that kittens up to six months of age may require being fed three meals a day, while most cats over 6 months of age will do fine with just two meals per day. Once your cat reaches its 7th year, you may feed them once day and maintain that routine. Only cats who have special food needs may be suggested more food intake per day.

Why is my cat always hungry?

This behavior can more commonly be observed in older cats. Here are some possible causes of excessive hunger:

- Cold weather
- Pregnancy
- Increased physical activities
- Low-quality food (these make the cat feel that it should eat some more to get the nutrition and satisfaction it needs.)
- Medicine intake
- Competition for food (if you have multiple cats at home.)
- Parasites in their intestines
- Diabetes
- Hyperthyroidism
- Cancer

It would be best not to jump into conclusions upon observing excessive hunger in your cat. It would be best to bring the cat to a vet for a proper examination. Also, do not overfeed your cat. Overfeeding results to obesity and this leads to worse health issues.

Which is better, dry food or wet cat food?

Below are the differences between dry food and wet food that could help you determine which you'd like to feed your cat:

Dry Food	Wet Food
Provides less nutrition.	More expensive than dry food.
Is composed of many "fillers" which can be harmful.	More appetizing than dry food.
Contains 10% of water.	Contains 70% of water.
Contains high amounts of Carbohydrates, which may cause obesity.	Some canned food cause dental problems such as gingivitis.

The verdict: Feeding your pet dry cat food is okay, as long as it is balanced. It could be better to ration the food rather than to free-feed. If your cat only eats dry food, make sure to encourage it to drink much water to avoid developing kidney stones.

Wet food or canned food on the other hand is always a good choice, but you must exercise control over the amount your cat eats. Since this type of food is more palatable than dry food, this can cause our cat to overeat.

Dr. Kallfelz states that mixing dry and wet food to make meals more appealing is not bad, but you have to make sure that you don't go over the ideal calorie intake of your cat. Your vet will be the best person to consult for a tailor-made meal plan that would best benefit your pet Chartreux.

Chapter Eight: Showing your Chartreux Cat

With its distinct look, it's no surprise why the Chartreux cat breed has been an officially recognized breed and is eligible for cat shows around the world. If you're up for the challenge, you can try presenting your pet Chartreux for pet shows for other cat enthusiasts to admire. The documents from your breeder can be of big help in determining whether your cat passes the qualifications of the Chartreux cat breed standard.

The Chartreux cat breed is recognized by the Cat Fanciers' Association (CFA) and is considered one of their "oldest new breeds," meaning, the Chartreux cat has been around for a long time, but has only been recognized and advanced to championship status in 1987.

The International Cat Association (TICA) also recognizes the Chartreux cat breed, making it eligible to compete in shows and earn appropriate titles. In TICA's top 25 winning cats, a Chartreux cat has earned the spot of "Tenth Best Kitten of the Year."

If you dream the same for your pet cat but don't know where to start, this chapter will outline everything you need to know about cat shows, presenting you pet Chartreux, and its breed standards.

The Chartreux Cat Breed Standard

Cat show breed standards and scoring systems are unique across cat show organizers such as the Cat Fanciers' Association (CFA) and The International Cat Association (TICA), but it helps to know the most common ones to determine early on if your cat is eligible or not.

Below are the general breed standards for the Chartreux cat:

General: The Chartreux cat must be sturdy and short-haired; it may even look primitive at times. Qualities such as intelligence, agility, and strength that are the core of the Chartreux's distinction must be evident during exhibitions.

Head and Neck:

- Must be broad and round but not spherical.
- Forehead is high and softly-contoured.
- Has full cheeks and powerful jaws, with male cats having bigger jowls.
- Nose is of medium width and length, and has a slight stop at eye-level.
- Muzzle is tapered with slight pads, giving it a sweet smiling expression. It must also be narrow and comparatively smaller than other breeds' noses.
- This breed's neck is short and its head, heavily-set.

Ears:

- Ears must have an erect posture, set high on the Chartreux cat's head.
- Size is medium in both height and width.

Eyes:

- Favored eye-color is a deep orange, but colors may also range from copper to gold.
- Eyes must be open and rounded, as if they are always attentive and communicative.

Body and Tail:

- Physique is full-bodied.
- Shoulders may be broad, medium or long.
- Chest is deep-set.
- Muscles are solid and dense.
- Bones are strong.
- Female cats are medium, while males are large.
- Moderately tall.
- Heavy at the base.
- Tail has an oval tip and is flexible and energetic.

Legs:

- Legs are straight and sturdy
- Fine-boned and comparatively short.

Feet:

- Round and medium-sized.
- May appear delicate compared to the Chartreux's full-bodied figure.

Coat:

- Coat may be medium or short in length.
- Woolly to the touch and should break similar to sheep skin at the neck and flanks.
- Top coat is protective.
- Undercoat is tough.
- Mature male Chartreux cats usually have the heaviest coats.
- Females and cats under two years may have thinner and silkier coats.

What you need to know about Cat Shows

Dog shows are probably more common than cat shows, but our feline friends deserve recognition, too! In ccat shows, judges compare cats to breed standards. These standards state how an ideal Charetreux cat looks and behaves.

Cats score higher when they are able to fulfill more breed standards set by the organizer. Breed standards are accurate, yet flexible. According to the CFA, the given standards aim to describe features that come from the natural style of the breed, but at times, judges also consider the proportion of the cat's overall features rather than whether they exactly conform to the measurements stated.

There are two types of cat shows according to the CFA:

- Specialty cat shows – Cats compete within a particular breed or color divisions.
- All-breed cat shows – Cats compete with other breeds.

In the CFA, separate shows run simultaneously throughout a hall, with rings for each judge. The process usually goes like this:

- Owners find their designated cage numbers and wait to be called.

- Once called, owners bring the cat to the cages in the different rings where the judges can inspect and rate them.

- Ring clerks and ring stewards are there to assist and make sure that numbers are called, records are maintained and cages are kept clean.

- Each judge is also accompanied by a master clerk.
- After examining all the cats in the all-breed or specialty shows, the judges tally the scores and present the top ten cats. Cat owners aim for their pet to be held "Best Cat in Show," but don't fret if you don't make it to the cut, your adorable pet Chartreux is special in its own way!

Awarding of Cat Show winners

Third place – Yellow ribbon

Second place – Red ribbon

First place – Blue ribbon

When a cat obtains six ribbons in the open category, it is declared as the champion and proceeds to compete with other champions. Champions who earn 200 points are then declared as the grand champion.

Being a Spectator in Cat Shows

Cat shows can be quite stressful for you and your Chartreux cat. If you want to compete in one, one advice is to attend a cat show first as a spectator, to get a feel of the event. You may want to read cat magazines and cat publications to know essential information about upcoming shows.

Here are some spectator guidelines on cat shows, according to the CFA:

- Spectators are requested not to touch the cats without permission from their owner to maintain the cleanliness of its coat. Do note that owners give their best efforts to show off their cats for the competition. Judges themselves wash their hands in between the inspection of each cat to prevent possible spreading of germs.

- Spectators may talk to judges and ask them questions whenever they are not busy handling or evaluating the cats. Remain on your seat and do not walk over to the rings if you want to ask questions.

- At times when you think that exhibitors are preoccupied, do not add to their stress by bombarding them with questions. Cat owners tend to be very busy during cat shows by listening for their numbers, announcements, and grooming their cat.

- Remember to ask for permission before taking photos of a cat in close-range. We do not advise the you use flash photography as this could stun and stress out the cats.

- Exhibitors wearing an "Ask Me" or "Ambassador" button would gladly answer your questions regarding the cat show. You may approach them anytime.

Entering a Cat Show with Your Pet Charteux

Determine first whether your cat will do fine in a busy environment and with strangers handling them to avoid stress. Once you are sure your Chartreux is up to the task, then it's time to understand the rules and prepare all necessary documents.

For The International Cat Association shows, the rules are as follows:

- All entries shall be accepted and received by the show's entry clerk, and there will be no limit to the number of entries for each category and show.

- Exhibitors may enter their kitten (a minimum of three months old) or their cat in the show for sale.

- Registration with TICA is a must for household pets.

- Pregnant cats are not allowed to compete.

- Cats' nails must be clipped before they are put on their bench. Declawed cats will not be penalized.

- The TICA show management provides a cage for each entry. Exhibitors may request for double cages and grooming areas for additional costs.

- Cage curtains are very important so that your cat will have privacy.

Classification of cats

For championship:

- Kittens (must be 4-8 calendar months of age)
- Adults (must be 8 calendar months of age once the show opens)
- Alters

For Household Pets:

- Kittens
- Adults

Things to bring during the show day

Prepare and pack all necessary items before the show to ensure a hassle-free experience. TICA lists down what you need to bring during the show day:

- Confirmation slip from the entry clerk
- All necessary grooming equipment
- Nail clippers
- Cage curtains
- A soft or comfortable bedding for the cat cage
- Your cat's pedigree and registration documents
- Proof of vaccination.

Guidelines during the show day

To make the experience memorable instead of stressful for you and your cat, here are some tips you should bear in mind:

- Be informed of the time the halls open and do your best to arrive early to prevent being stuck in long check-in lines.
- Prepare your confirmation slips upon check-in.
- Once you've received your number, keep it secured and do not lose it.
- Check your entry information in the show catalogue and immediately inform the Master Clerk if there are any mistakes in your information.
- Familiarize yourself with the different judging rings and check your schedule so that you do not get lost or late once your pet Chartreux is called to any of the rings.
- Immediately find your bench, set up the curtains, and help your cat feel settled. This is ideal to prevent undue stress before the judging starts.

Here are some do's and don'ts for exhibitors:

- Do clip the nails of your cat before benching. There is a possibility of disqualification, should you fail to do this.

- Do observe care and caution towards cats and other exhibitors at all times.

- Prior to being called in the ring, inform the ring clerk if your cat needs special caging to avoid delaying judging and causing inconvenience to judges and other exhibitors.
- Don't tell the judges which among the cats in the ring is your entry.

- Don't request for your entry to be judged separately from other entries.

- Unless requested by the judges, do not linger in the ring and hold your cat out once it is called for judging.

Note: The judges only know the following information about your entry during the show day:

- Breed
- Entry number

- Sex
- Age on show day
- Category / division
- Colors and patterns.

Judges don't have any other info about your cat, including their status and awards, nor do they have any information about the owners.

Training Your Cat for a Show

Cat show judges inspect not only how your entry looks, but also how it behaves and responds. Training your pet Chartreux before a show could be of great help in earning better scores in the judges' books.

One important thing to keep in mind is not be harsh in training your pet. Use rewards to encourage your cat during training time and always be patient to obtain desirable behavior.

Some tips for adult cat training include:

- **Teaching your cat to stand erect with a good posture.** Although it is more difficult to teach cats to "sit" and "stand" than dogs, try to train your pet Chartreux to do these for a few moments. The judges will be impressed. Reward your cat with gentle nose strokes downward whenever it is in good posture.

- **Ask an expert to train your cat prior to a show.** The CFA created a mentorship program where newbies can be accustomed to the process in cat shows.

On the other hand, kitten training may involve more dynamic processes such as these:

- Have the kitten get used to being carried on your forearms and hands. The earlier you start carrying them comfortably, the better they will feel once the show day arrives.

- Put the kitten on unfamiliar surfaces such as your lap, a desk, or even on the grooming table and play with them to make them feel confident being in these surfaces.

- Find a toy that the kitten likes and teach it to jump up to touch the toy.

- For kittens, bathing is advised every 3 weeks, down to two, and then weekly when the show day is one month away.

- You may slowly introduce the kitten to new people and friends so that it does not develop a shy or easily frightened attitude.

During the show day, play with your kitten and offer it treats to keep it as happy and relaxed as possible. If allowed, you may also bring the kitten out to a show table to familiarize it with the sounds and the smells that surround it.

Chapter Nine: Keeping Chartreux Cats Healthy

You've probably waited quite some time to finally be able to bring home your pet Chartreux that you want to know the most effective ways to keep it in top shape. One sure way to keep a cat happy is ensuring that it is getting all the resources it needs to grow healthy and strong. No cat is perfect, but fortunately for you, the Chartreux is a generally healthy breed.

Diseases in cats are commonly genetic, meaning, health risks vary among the different breeds of cats. Thankfully, much has been researched about this and you can now be fully aware of threats to their health even before they arrive in your home.

Knowing the Chartreux's health concerns will help you prepare the best health plans for them. Knowing what health risks to expect is essential to becoming a good and responsible pet owner.

Whether you are taking care of a kitten or an older cat, you must watch out for the same health risks that can threaten their life. Some infectious diseases affect kittens more seriously than it does adults. New born kittens may get immunity from their mother until eight weeks old, so consult a veterinarian for the best vaccinations and health practices for your cat. Also make sure that you are getting your Chartreux cat only from reputable breeders.

Chapter 9 outlines some of the most common health problems of Chartreux cats, as well as how to manage it and help them live a normal, happy life despite their condition. This chapter will also tackle tips to help you do your part in controlling your cat's health and save them from the most common cat health problems such as obesity. Remember, the healthier you keep your Chartreux cat, the longer you will have an affectionate companion at home. Keep every member of the family (cat included!) happy by being a responsible pet owner!

An Overview of the Chartreux Cat's health

Chartreux cats have been found to have less genetic problems than other breeds, but they are not free from illness and health risks. Some health concerns observed in this breed are:

- Patellar (knee cap) luxation
- Obesity

Those mentioned above might seem discouraging, but you'll be surprised to know that one of these risks can be prevented simply by watching your pet's diet, just how you watch over your own.

Because knowledge is power, we've gathered the most essential information you need to know about these health risks, to be prepared early on!

Patellar Luxation

The Patella, commonly known as the kneecap, is a protective bone that covers the front of the stifle. This small, thick bone can be found humans as well as in animals such as cats, birds, and mice. You can find the Patella firmly attached to tendons and ligaments within the cat's knee joints and serves its purpose whenever a cat bends or straightens its knees.

Complications involving the Patella can either be caused by genetic defects (related to the cat's breed) or sharp physical trauma. The Chatreux cat breed is no stranger to a complication called "Patellar Luxation," or having their kneecap out of place.

Symptoms:

Chartreux cats with a luxating Patella will shows signs of abnormal hindlimb movement when walking or running. This can also be observed when a cat is suddenly having difficulty in jumping.

Oftentimes though, a cat will not show signs of pain or discomfort until the condition is in its advanced stage. Lameness, in the sense that the cat is having trouble walking because of an unusual feeling in its kneecap, can be observed as the cat gets older.

Causes:

As for the Chartreux cat breed, it is believed that Patellar luxation is caused by genetic defects. Some enthusiiasts say that the Chartreux cat breed's ability to put on weight and grow a big, bulky body, which may be a bit heavy for their fine-boned legs to support may take a toll on their kneecap, causing it to pop out. Other findings also suggest that Patellar luxation is inherited, and developmental problems in joints appear to have complex inheritance patterns.

Diagnosis

Your cat's veterinarians perform an examination by touching and feel the kneecap for any signs of displacement. The vet may also recommend mediolateral (side view) and crainocaudal (top view) x-rays of your Chatreux cat's hip, hock, and stifle joint.

Another test that may be done is by taking synovial fluid (a lubricating fluid) samples from the joint. A cat with Patellar luxation will have a small increase in mononuclear cells.

Vets classify patients into four grades:

- *Grade 1* – This is the least severe condition, wherein the Patella can effortlessly return to its normal position when released, despite being easily moved.

- *Grades 2-3* – Being classified in this grade means that the severity of the cat's kneecap luxation varies between least severe to most severe.

- *Grade 4* – In this grade, the Patella is found out to be displaced all the time and it cannot be manually put back into its normal position.

The grading system helps doctors determine whether a pet is a candidate for surgery. Pets in grades 1-2 usually hop or skip at times due to discomfort, and may also episodes of lameness, but they are likely to learn how to pop their own kneecap back into place. Patients in grades 3-4, however, may strongly be advised to undergo surgery because severe Patellar luxation can lead to prolonged lameness, or worse, being totally unable to use the affected leg.

Treatment

Surgery for this condition usually involves excavating the trochlear groove so that the patella stays in place, and adding stability by tightening the capsule and soft tissues around the affected joints of the cat.

Recover after surgery is usually rapid, as long as pet owners follow the Veterinarian's instructions regarding bandaging and mild, appropriate exercise. You may also be advised to prevent your cat from moving too much to let the affected area heal quicker.

Obesity

Obesity is one of the leading causes of more chronic illnesses and deaths in cats. Although this is a commonly known fact, a lot of pet owners still do not take the dangers of improper weight management seriously. The last thing we'd want is a cat having a hard time moving around because its body is already too heavy, oddly enough; we still notice many household cats who are obviously looking overweight and unhealthy.

Symptoms:

Excessive weight-gain and body fat build-up is one of the most common things you may notice in an obese cat. Also, if you'd try to pat either side of your cat's tummy, you should be able to feel its ribs, if not, then the cat may be overweight.

You may also want to look out for swinging pouches on your cat's hind legs, as this is another part of their body where you can excessive fat storage.

Obese cats often have trouble cleaning some parts of their body, so if you check your Chartreux cat's anal area and find that it is dirty, then it could be a sign of obesity.

Causes:

Over-nourishment causes excessive fat to build up in the cat's body. You may think that a chubby cat is cute, but if yours is not fond of exercise and other physical activities, your Chartreux cat can easily gain weight. Obesity is the result of imbalance energy storage and usage. Giving your cat much treats throughout the day may seem like a good idea, but frequent treat-giving, along with feeding the cat a high-calorie diet may lead to obesity.

Diagnosis:

A veterinarian will examine your cat's rib, lumbar, head, and tail areas to assess its body composition. The vet will compare the results to the Chartreux cat breed standards, and if your cat's body condition goes over seven, then there's a chance that it is obese.

Treatment:

Weight-loss programs involving a change in diet and increased exercise is the best way to help your cat lose weight. With proper health management, your cat could ideally lose one pound per month.

Your feeding habits will greatly affect your cat's recovery and weight loss. Cut on the high-calorie diet and switch to low-calorie cat food. Feeding your cat the same amount of food served in smaller portions throughout the day may be more effective in burning calories. Always consult with your veterinarian before making changes to your cat's diet, crash-diets will surely upset their stomach and could result to bigger problems in the long run.

Physical activities are also essential for your cat's weight loss. Encourage your pet Chartreux to move around by playing with it or taking it outside to climb a tree. This breed usually likes toys it can chase, so look for moving mouse toys or make your own toy by simply attaching feathers on a stick! It can be simple, but you'll have to do your part to help your cat maintain its health. Remember that even mild obesity can shorten your cat's lifespan.

Grooming a Chartreux cat

Proper grooming is essential in order to maintain its beautiful blue-gray fur and overall well-being. Although Chartreux cats can clean themselves well, you still have to take them on trips to a trusted groomer to make sure that they are in top shape.

Here are some guidelines in grooming a Chartreux cat:

- Combing, not brushing, is what a Chartreux's coat really needs. You may run your fingers through its coat to prevent matting. In seasons of shedding (which happens several in fall or spring for this breed), you may want to comb through its undercoat daily to control the shedding.

- Often check your pet Chartreux's ear for foul odor and dirt build-up. They can usually clean this area by themselves, but you can help them by using a damp cotton ball and gently rubbing inside to collect dirt and debris. A cat with clean ears is a healthy cat!

- The Chartreux cat has a water-repellant undercoat, meaning, it will be difficult to wet the fur and its body as well. Luckily, Chartreux cats don't need much bathing; once a week in the tub will suffice. Patience is key when bathing your pet.

- Brushing its teeth is also important. Consult with a vet for your cat's dental health. All breeds of cats are susceptible to dental problems, but you can minimize the risk of acquiring it with regular brushing.

- Nail-trimming prevents your cat from accidentally wounding both human and animal companions, and can help prevent damage on your home furniture. If you are not confident trimming its nails yourself, you may take your pet Chartreux to a groomer and have it done there to avoid wounding its paws.

Training Your Chartreux cat

The Chartreux loves playtime! This quality makes them an excellent pet for households with kids. Some of their favorite activities are playing fetch and tag as well as chasing toys. We can't say for sure what other tricks these adorable cats can pull off, but you can always try teaching them!

Things to remember when training your cat to do tricks:

- Prepare low-calorie treats that you can give them whenever they accomplish something.

- Do not be harsh in disciplining or teaching them tricks. This breed is known to be highly sensitive to punishment and harsh training. Try giving them positive reinforcement so as not to discourage them.

- Chartreux cats enjoy short durations of playtime. You may find it odd that they are running around one minute and napping at the next. This is a normal behavior for them, so do not force them long hours of playtime.

Should I spay or neuter my Chartreux cat?

Veterinarians strongly suggest that owners spay or neuter their cats. Neutering is found to have a lot of benefits including the correction of bad behavior such as territorial spraying, aggression, and roaming, which are common for male cats.

Female cats can also be observed to have better behavior after surgery. If they are spayed between 3 to 6 months, you could protect them from mammary cancer and from an infection of the uterus called pyometra, which usually affects older female cats.

Spaying and Neutering Costs

Operations at full-service veterinary clinics may cost you around $200 for a male cat, and $300 up to $500 for a female cat. Don't fret, for non-profit spay or neuter services could charge as low as $50, and may vary according to your location. Only licensed veterinarians are allowed to perform these surgeries.

The American Society for the Prevention of Cruelty to Animals (ASPCA) and Humane Society has lists of low-cost spay and neuter programs on their websites.

Chapter Ten: Care Sheet and Summary

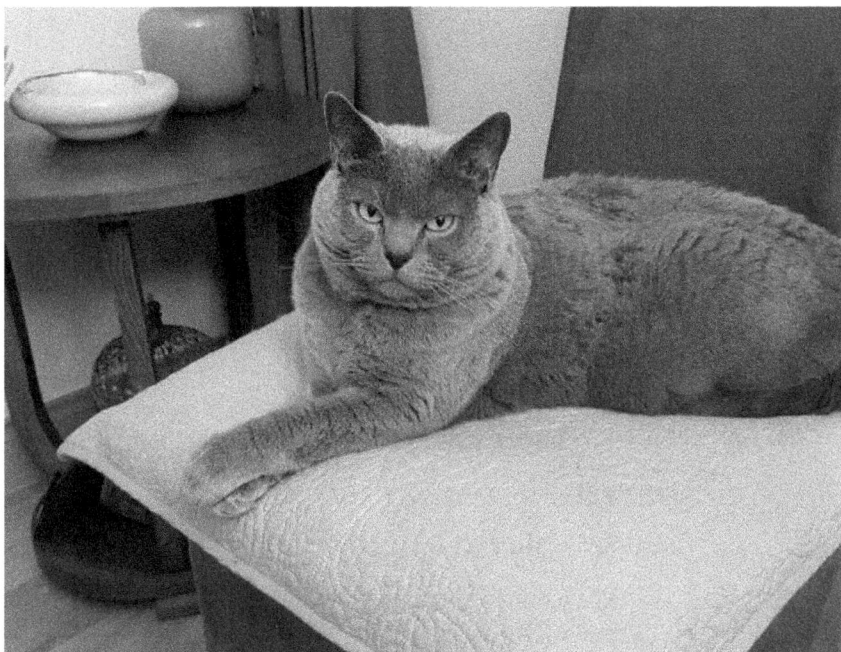

Here's a quick summary of all the things you need to know when it comes to keeping a Chartreux Cat. We've highlighted the basic pet keeping guide as well as some general information for your new potential pet so that you can do a quick browse even if you're on the go!

We hope this guide book has helped you decide whether or not you're ready in taking the responsibility of keeping cats in general. Make sure to share this with your friends and apply all the steps and lessons you've gathered from this book. Happy cat keeping!

Physical Traits

Head and facial features:

- The Chartreux has narrow, tapered muzzle
- They also have a powerful-looking jaw, which sets them apart from other gray-colored breeds.
- Chartreux cats usually have brilliant orange or copper eyes that are so expressive
- The Chartreux's nose, like its ears are medium-sized.
- Their ears stand erect high on their head, making them look alert at all times.

Body:

- Female Chartreux cats are usually medium-sized, weighing 6 to 11 pounds, while males grow larger, between 10-16 pounds.
- Chartreux cats grow moderately tall, which makes them agile and less clumsy.

Coat:

- The Chartreux's coat is water-repellant and is noticeably woolly.

- They also have pretty dense undercoats that make the perfect protection from various elements.
- Females may have silkier and slightly thinner fur, while mature male Chartreux cats boast heavy coats.

Behavioral Traits

- Unlike other prominent breeds, Chartreux cats are generally silent—the only time you'd probably hear them vocalize their thoughts is when something greatly interests them
- Chartreux cats are communicative and friendly.
- They aren't very demanding, but they would enjoy following you around, observing the things you do, and occasionally bumping their head on your feet as a sign of affection.
- Chartreux cats easily get along with family members of all ages because of their good nature.
- At times, Chartreux cats may exhibit dog-like behavior like learning to play fetch and responding when its name is called!

What makes the Charteux cat breed a great pet?

General temperament:

- o Loyal but independent
- o Adaptable and friendly
- o Quiet but communicative

Pros and Cons of Owning a Chartreux Cat

PROs

- Chartreux cats make great family cats.
- Easily gets along with other pets.
- The Chartreux is known to be a healthy cat breed
- This breed only has few grooming requirements.
- Their short coat makes it easy to care for them.

CONs

- Chartreux cat owners must look out for tendencies of Patellar Luxation or a popping knee cap.
- Diet must be strictly controlled as this breed is thick and large. Overfeeding results to obesity that is bad for the Chartreux thin legs.

- This breed's water-repellant coat makes it difficult to get it wet down to the skin when bathing.
- The Chartreux is a very rare cat breed, so extensive research is required for you to find a reputable Chartreux cat breeder.

Legal Requirements

USA

- Some municipal ordinances may require proof of vaccination and identification.
- Cats are not required to wear collars in the U.S. as it is believed to go against their nature. It is, however, good for cats get used to wearing collars for reasons other than looking extra cute:
  o Easy identification
  o It can serve as an alert for cats with medical conditions.

UK

- The new law states that license exemptions for people who repeatedly sell kittens that are bred from non-pedigree cats will be removed, and there will be stricter conditions for breeder licenses to be approved.

- Since the U.K. has successfully eliminated Rabies in 1922, your cat may be required to undergo a quarantine period as a strict safety measure.

Travelling With Your Pet

- The customs require, pet owners to indicate animals travelling with them in their declaration documents.
- In the U.S., various states may impose their own regulations on interstate animal transportation, so it will be best to get in touch with the local government of the municipality you're planning to head to first before traveling.

The Ideal Home for Cats

- DO make sure that there will be hiding spots
- DO make litter trays, water bowl, and food bowls easily accessible
- DO maximize vertical space
- DO keep containers closed at all times.
- DO provide comfortable bedding
- DON'T encourage your cat to nap near hot surfaces like stoves or fireplaces.
- DO allot one litter tray for 1-2 cats only.

- DON'T leave hazardous and poisonous chemicals exposed.
- DO buy your Chartreux cat some toys to keep it busy.
- DON'T leave cords and strings dangling.
- DO tape and secure electrical wiring properly.
- DON'T keep toxic plants at home.

Environmental Enrichment

Here are some tips to achieve an enriched environment for cats at home:

- Stimulate their senses.
- Incorporate natural feeding methods every once in a while.

Living in a multi-cat home

PROs

- Decreased signs of behavior problems.
- Grooming made easier.
- Happier cats = happier home.

CONs

- More paws could mean more trouble.

- It is time-consuming.
- Expenses are doubled.

Home Equipment You'll Need for Chartreux Cats

The Basic Needs of Chartreux cats

- Food and Water Bowls
- Kitty Litter
- Bedding
- Toys
- Cat Furniture
- Cat Enclosures

Tips in Setting Up the Home Equipment

- Choose an ideal location
- Accessibility to humans
- Consider the age of your cat
- Evaluate your budget

Feeding Your Chartreux Cat

- **Minerals** – Minerals are involved in most of a cat's physiological reactions like pH balance, enzyme formulation, oxygen transportation, and nutrient utilization.

- **Protein** – Cats need a great amount of protein in their body.
- **Vitamins** – Vitamins are important to our pets as it is for us humans.
- **Water** – Cats have low levels of thirst because they can fulfill much of their water requirements by eating fresh, raw food.
- **Fatty Acids** - These nutrients are involved with metabolism functions and cell integrity in a cat's body.

Showing Your Chartreux Cat

General Breed Standard: The Chartreux cat must be sturdy and short-haired; it may even look primitive at times. Qualities such as intelligence, agility, and strength that are the core of the Chartreux's distinction must be evident during exhibitions.

There are two types of cat shows according to the CFA:

- Specialty cat shows – Cats compete within a particular breed or color divisions.

- All-breed cat shows – Cats compete with other breeds.

Awarding of Cat Show Winners

o Third place – Yellow ribbon
o Second place – Red ribbon
o First place – Blue ribbon

Classification of cats

For championship:

- Kittens (must be 4-8 calendar months of age)
- Adults (must be 8 calendar months of age once the show opens)
- Alters

For Household Pets:

- Kittens
- Adults

Things to bring during the show day

- Confirmation slip from the entry clerk
- All necessary grooming equipment
- Nail clippers
- Cage curtains
- A soft or comfortable bedding for the cat cage
- Your cat's pedigree and registration documents
- Proof of vaccination.

Keeping Chartreux Cats Healthy

An Overview of the Chartreux Cat's health

Patellar Luxation

The Patella, commonly known as the kneecap, is a protective bone that covers the front of the stifle.

- **Symptoms**

  Chartreux cats with a luxating Patella will shows signs of abnormal hindlimb movement when walking or running.

- **Treatment**

  Surgery for this condition usually involves excavating the trochlear groove so that the patella stays in place, and adding stability by tightening the capsule and soft tissues around the affected joints of the cat.

Obesity

Obesity is one of the leading causes of more chronic illnesses and deaths in cats.

- o **Symptoms**

  Excessive weight-gain and body fat build-up is one of the most common things you may notice in an obese cat.

- o **Treatment**

  Weight-loss programs involving a change in diet and increased exercise is the best way to help your cat lose weight.

Glossary of Cat Terms

Abundism – Referring to a cat that has markings more prolific than is normal.

Acariasis – A type of mite infection.

ACF – Australian Cat Federation

Affix – A cattery name that follows the cat's registered name; cattery owner, not the breeder of the cat.

Agouti – A type of natural coloring pattern in which individual hairs have bands of light and dark coloring.

Ailurophile – A person who loves cats.

Albino – A type of genetic mutation which results in little to no pigmentation, in the eyes, skin, and coat.

Allbreed – Referring to a show that accepts all breeds or a judge who is qualified to judge all breeds.

Alley Cat – A non-pedigreed cat.

Alter – A desexed cat; a male cat that has been neutered or a female that has been spayed.

Amino Acid – The building blocks of protein; there are 22 types for cats, 11 of which can be synthesized and 11 which must come from the diet (see essential amino acid).

Anestrus – The period between estrus cycles in a female cat.

Any Other Variety (AOV) – A registered cat that doesn't conform to the breed standard.

ASH – American Shorthair, a breed of cat.

Back Cross – A type of breeding in which the offspring is mated back to the parent.

Balance – Referring to the cat's structure; proportional in accordance with the breed standard.

Barring – Describing the tabby's striped markings.

Base Color – The color of the coat.

Bicolor – A cat with patched color and white.

Blaze – A white coloring on the face, usually in the shape of an inverted V.

Bloodline – The pedigree of the cat.

Brindle – A type of coloring, a brownish or tawny coat with streaks of another color.

Castration – The surgical removal of a male cat's testicles.

Cat Show – An event where cats are shown and judged.

Cattery – A registered cat breeder; also, a place where cats may be boarded.

CFA – The Cat Fanciers Association.

Cobby – A compact body type.

Colony – A group of cats living wild outside.

Color Point – A type of coat pattern that is controlled by color point alleles; pigmentation on the tail, legs, face, and ears with an ivory or white coat.

Colostrum – The first milk produced by a lactating female; contains vital nutrients and antibodies.

Conformation – The degree to which a pedigreed cat adheres to the breed standard.

Cross Breed – The offspring produced by mating two distinct breeds.

Dam – The female parent.

Declawing – The surgical removal of the cat's claw and first toe joint.

Developed Breed – A breed that was developed through selective breeding and crossing with established breeds.

Down Hairs – The short, fine hairs closest to the body which keep the cat warm.

DSH – Domestic Shorthair.

Estrus – The reproductive cycle in female cats during which she becomes fertile and receptive to mating.

Fading Kitten Syndrome – Kittens that die within the first two weeks after birth; the cause is generally unknown.

Feral – A wild, untamed cat of domestic descent.

Gestation – Pregnancy; the period during which the fetuses develop in the female's uterus.

Guard Hairs – Coarse, outer hairs on the coat.

Harlequin – A type of coloring in which there are van markings of any color with the addition of small patches of the same color on the legs and body.

Inbreeding – The breeding of related cats within a closed group or breed.

Kibble – Another name for dry cat food.

Lilac – A type of coat color that is pale pinkish-gray.

Line – The pedigree of ancestors; family tree.

Litter – The name given to a group of kittens born at the same time from a single female.

Mask – A type of coloring seen on the face in some breeds.

Matts – Knots or tangles in the cat's fur.

Mittens – White markings on the feet of a cat.

Moggie – Another name for a mixed breed cat.

Mutation – A change in the DNA of a cell.

Muzzle – The nose and jaws of an animal.

Natural Breed – A breed that developed without selective breeding or the assistance of humans.

Neutering – Desexing a male cat.

Open Show – A show in which spectators are allowed to view the judging.

Pads – The thick skin on the bottom of the feet.

Particolor – A type of coloration in which there are markings of two or more distinct colors.

Patched – A type of coloration in which there is any solid color, tabby, or tortoiseshell color plus white.

Pedigree – A purebred cat; the cat's papers showing its family history.

Pet Quality – A cat that is not deemed of high enough standard to be shown or bred.

Piebald – A cat with white patches of fur.

Points – Also color points; markings of contrasting color on the face, ears, legs, and tail.

Pricked – Referring to ears that sit upright.

Purebred – A pedigreed cat.

Queen – An intact female cat.

Roman Nose – A type of nose shape with a bump or arch.

Scruff – The loose skin on the back of a cat's neck.

Selective Breeding – A method of modifying or improving a breed by choosing cats with desirable traits.

Senior – A cat that is more than 5 but less than 7 years old.

Sire – The male parent of a cat.

Solid – Also self; a cat with a single coat color.

Spay – Desexing a female cat.

Stud – An intact male cat.

Tabby – A type of coat pattern consisting of a contrasting color over a ground color.

Tom Cat – An intact male cat.

Tortoiseshell – A type of coat pattern consisting of a mosaic of red or cream and another base color.

Tri-Color – A type of coat pattern consisting of three distinct colors in the coat.

Tuxedo – A black and white cat.

Unaltered – A cat that has not been desexed.

Index

A

amino acid 106
antibodies..108

B

body...108, 109
breed 107, 108, 109, 110, 111
breeder 106, 107
breeding 107, 108, 109, 110

C

Cat Fanciers Association 108
cattery 106
CFA...108
claw..108
coat 106, 107, 108, 109, 111
color.. 107, 108, 109, 110, 111
cycle 109

D

desexed 106, 111
diet...106
DNA...110
domestic...109

E

ears 108, 110
essential 106

estrus 107

F

face 107, 108, 109, 110
family 109, 110
feet 109, 110
female 106, 107, 108, 109, 111
fertile 109
food 109
fur 109, 110

G

genetic 106

I

infection 106
intact 111

J

judge 106

K

kittens 109

L

lactating 108

M

male 106, 107, 110, 111

markings 106, 107, 109, 110

milk 108

mite 106

mutation.. 106

N

neutered... 106

nose 110, 111

nutrients.. 108

O

offspring 107, 108

P

pattern.. 106, 108, 111

pedigree 107, 109

pigmentation.. 106, 108

protein... 106

purebred.. 110

S

show 106, 110

skin.. 106, 110, 111

standard 107, 108, 110

T

tail 108, 110

traits 111

Photo Credits

Page 1 Photo by user bDom – artiste via Flickr.com,
https://www.flickr.com/photos/bdom/34070578771/

Page 4 Photo by user Banehtnha Nabnoba via Flickr.com,
https://www.flickr.com/photos/134585064@N05/24819205065
/
Page 13 Photo by user N'Grid via Flickr.com,
https://www.flickr.com/photos/vivalivadia/8489462528/

Page 28 Photo by user Max Sat via Flickr.com,
https://www.flickr.com/photos/96092563@N08/23673733646/

Page 47 Photo by user bDom – artiste via Flickr.com,
https://www.flickr.com/photos/bdom/31978350364/

Page 54 Photo by user Mike McCune via Flickr.com,
https://www.flickr.com/photos/mccun934/4935826791/

Page 63 Photo by user Thomas via Flickr.com,
https://www.flickr.com/photos/38746820@N07/15823925898/

Page 72 Photo by user bDom – artiste via Flickr.com,
https://www.flickr.com/photos/bdom/15921575846/

Page 89 Photo by user bDom – artiste via Flickr.com,
https://www.flickr.com/photos/bdom/32667739422/

Page 103 Photo by user LucEdouard via Flickr.com,
https://www.flickr.com/photos/lucedouard/33650147324/

References

"Becoming a cat breeder" Siamese-cat-breeder.co.uk

http://www.siamese-cat-breeder.co.uk/10-questions-to-ask-yourself-before-becoming-a-cat-breeder/

"How to know a good breeder" purrinlot.com

https://www.purrinlot.com/how-to-know-a-good-breeder.htm

"15 Questions to ask cat breeders" petplace.com

https://www.petplace.com/article/cats/pet-care/15-questions-you-should-ask-cat-breeders/

"Chartreux Cat Breed Standards" cfa.org

http://cfa.org/Portals/0/documents/breeds/standards/chartreux.pdf

"Helping your cat adjust to a new home" paws.org

https://www.paws.org/library/cats/home-life/helping-your-cat-adjust/

"Introducing your cat to a new cat" paws.org

https://www.paws.org/library/cats/home-life/introducing-cat-to-cat/

"Introducing cats to a new home" georgiaspca.org

http://www.georgiaspca.org/qa-sfspca-intro-cat-to-new-home

"The pro's and con's of multiple cats" wisconsinpetcare.com

https://wisconsinpetcare.com/the-pros-and-cons-of-multiple-cats/

"Are you ready for a new cat?" momtastic.com

http://www.momtastic.com/life/173475-one-cat-or-more-benefits-and-challenges-of-a-multi-cat-home/

"General Health Information for your Chartreux" aubreyamc.com

http://aubreyamc.com/feline/chartreux/

"Chartreux Cat Information" cattime.com

http://cattime.com/cat-breeds/chartreux-cats#/slide/1

"Chartreux Cat Breed Profile" cfa.org

http://cfa.org/Breeds/BreedsCJ/Chartreux.aspx

"Chartreux Cat Information and Personality Traits" hillspet.com

https://www.hillspet.com/cat-care/cat-breeds/chartreux

"Luxating Patella in Cats" vcahospitals.com

https://vcahospitals.com/know-your-pet/luxating-patella-in-cats

"Obesity in Cats" petmd.com

https://www.petmd.com/cat/conditions/digestive/c_ct_obesity

"Feeding your Cat" vet.cornell.edu

http://www.vet.cornell.edu/fhc/Health_Information/brochure_feedingcat.cfm

"Food that are dangerous or toxic to cats" hillspet.com

https://www.hillspet.com/cat-care/nutrition-feeding/toxic-foods-for-cats

"DIY Build an Outdoor Cat Enclosure in 5 Easy Steps" organicauthority.com

http://www.organicauthority.com/pets/diy-build-outdoor-cat-enclosure.html

"Cat Equipment Basics" vetbabble.com

https://www.vetbabble.com/cats/getting-started-cats/cat-equipment-basics/

"My olds cat is always hungry, what could be wrong?" bbbvet.org.uk

http://www.bbbvet.org.uk/my-old-cat-is-always-hungry-what-could-be-wrong/

"Entering a cat show" animals.hostuffworks.com

http://www.bbbvet.org.uk/my-old-cat-is-always-hungry-what-could-be-wrong/

"How to train a cat for show" animals.mom.me

http://animals.mom.me/how-to-train-a-cat-for-a-show-12112470.html

"Kitten training for show" purrinlot.com

http://animals.mom.me/how-to-train-a-cat-for-a-show-12112470.html

"The Wet cat food VS Dry Cat Food debate" catster.com

http://www.catster.com/cat-food/cat-food-wet-or-dry

"Enclosures for cats" communityconcernforcats.org

http://www.communityconcernforcats.org/resources/enclosures-for-cats/

Feeding Baby
Cynthia Cherry
978-1941070000

Axolotl
Lolly Brown
978-0989658430

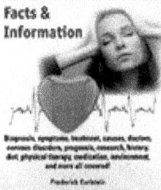

Dysautonomia, POTS
Syndrome
Frederick Earlstein
978-0989658485

Degenerative Disc
Disease Explained
Frederick Earlstein
978-0989658485

Sinusitis, Hay Fever,
Allergic Rhinitis Explained
Frederick Earlstein
978-1941070024

Wicca
Riley Star
978-1941070130

Zombie Apocalypse
Rex Cutty
978-1941070154

Capybara
Lolly Brown
978-1941070062

Eels As Pets
Lolly Brown
978-1941070167

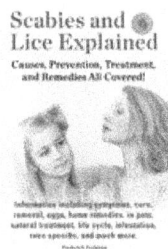

Scabies and Lice Explained
Frederick Earlstein
978-1941070017

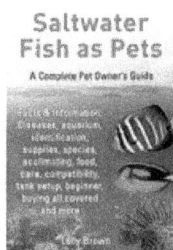

Saltwater Fish As Pets
Lolly Brown
978-0989658461

Torticollis Explained
Frederick Earlstein
978-1941070055

Kennel Cough
Lolly Brown
978-0989658409

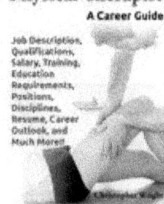

Physiotherapist, Physical
Therapist
Christopher Wright
978-0989658492

Rats, Mice, and Dormice
As Pets
Lolly Brown
978-1941070079

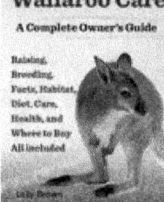

Wallaby and Wallaroo Care
Lolly Brown
978-1941070031

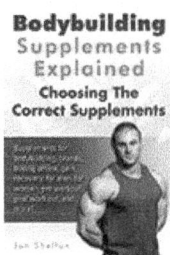

Bodybuilding Supplements
Explained
Jon Shelton
978-1941070239

Demonology
Riley Star
978-19401070314

Pigeon Racing
Lolly Brown
978-1941070307

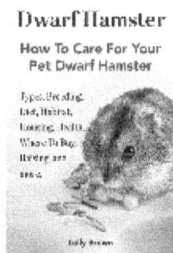

Dwarf Hamster
Lolly Brown
978-1941070390

Cryptozoology
Rex Cutty
978-1941070406

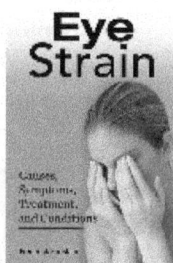

Eye Strain
Frederick Earlstein
978-1941070369

Inez The Miniature Elephant
Asher Ray
978-1941070353

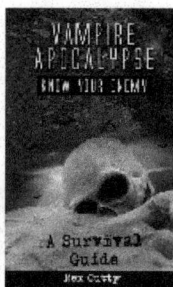

Vampire Apocalypse
Rex Cutty
978-1941070321

www.ingramcontent.com/pod-product-compliance
Lightning Source LLC
Chambersburg PA
CBHW052108090426
42741CB00009B/1729

* 9 7 8 1 9 4 6 2 8 6 7 3 4 *